"TOIT"

The success of a plan or a project
Depends on just how well you do it;
But the <u>doing</u> depends
- from beginning to end -
On one plain, simple fact: you got <u>to it</u>!

*****

ISBN 0-9637778-0-7

Produced by ERTIA UNLIMITED
P.O. BOX 23516
LEXINGTON, KY 40523-3516

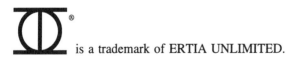

CONTENTS

(contents cont'd)

ACKNOWLEDGEMENTS

This work would not have materialized without the support and encouragement of the following individuals who are recognized with deepest appreciation:

DARREN KELLY
For painstaking graphic representations of symbols.

ANDREW KELLY
For computer program interpolation.

ERIC DURBIN
For computing resource management and oversight,
plus great patience in files management instruction.

B. EUGENE GRIESSMAN
For persistent encouragement and impeccable advice.

Finally, I wish to acknowledge my family, co-workers and numerous ad hoc consultants for their good-humored indulgence through every insufferable "TOITISM"!

"The most compelling factor in progress is a sense of urgency."

Composite Observation

PREFACE

One of the most basic facts and faults of life is that certain things <u>don't</u> happen that <u>should</u> happen because <u>nobody gets around to doing them</u>. Behind every success is the fact that <u>somebody finally got around to it</u>.

Gimmicks to remind us of the need for action (e.g., "Getting A ROUND TUIT") have surfaced in variant forms over the past 20-25 years. Those I have seen personally are round buttons or paperweights with the inscriptions "TOIT" or "TUIT".

However, a more intrinsically encapsulating symbol for this concept seemed needed that would use only the basic elements of the letters T/O/I/T. The most direct representation — achieved simply by combining the letters frontwards, backwards and upside down — turned out to be the most versatile and was "christened" the BASIC TOIT. A plethora of associated TOIT concepts quickly followed, bringing unique contributions to the universal challenges of entropy, Murphy's Laws, and inertia. Brief annotations were added to delineate their respective roles in optimizing progress.

At some point in the process, the symbols began to exceed the sublime, with important subtleties lost in the physical rendering. But there were such important TOITs to be included that the listings and annotations continued, using an "open" TOIT symbol as a general representation for concepts not otherwise easily represented.

The listings contained herein are obviously incomplete by a wide margin. But they provide a series of beginning reference points to help along the way to success. As you will see, the TOITs have been fun, philosophically challenging, and amazingly versatile for all their simplicity.

For all of those TOITs unsymboled or unlisted which may, nonetheless, be important, it is intended that the BASIC TOIT symbol will serve as the fundamentally inclusive reminder of things most necessary to assure success. May those successes in your own experience be many and may you enjoy getting there — hopefully a little easier and/or more directly — with the help of a platoon of TOITs along the way!

"Extraordinary accomplishments arise from the EXTRAORDINARY determination and efforts of ordinary persons."

*****

CONTRASTING FORCES

The "push-pull" essence of life has been a challenge ever since Eve discovered the apple. Early Chinese philosophers described a duality of opposing life forces which they named YIN and YANG, depicted by the symbol below.

Such contrasting forces must be clearly recognized and skillfully (PAINSTAKINGLY!) managed to achieve ultimate success.

"Only two kinds of problems ever reach my desk — those marked 'urgent' and those marked 'important' — and I spend so much time on the 'urgent' I never get to the 'important'."

Dwight D. Eisenhower [1]

CHALLENGES OF THE FIRST KIND

INERTIA

Projects often seem much more difficult to start than they are to carry out. This natural phenomenon is known as the "Law of Inertia": Anything not already underway tends never to get there unless imposed upon by a force of sufficient magnitude to get it moving. Similarly, it is difficult to change direction or halt a process which has significant momentum [including that of time, money or ego already invested].

MURPHY'S LAW and THERMODYNAMICS (the Second Law)

"If anything CAN go wrong, it WILL."

"Anything left to itself tends toward the state of greatest disorder."

No matter how you color it, misfortunes and natural attrition abound. Nothing is guaranteed except that opportunities come and go but challenges accumulate.

DISTRACTION

Competing priorities (either real or imagined) and various "happenstance" occurrences can command a semblance of intrinsic merit — if only just for the moment — sufficient to cause a faltering break in stride on more central matters, even for the most organized and highly motivated managers. Add a social consciousness or sensitivity and one will occasionally permit (or even invite) interruptions by coworkers. Such diversions/distractions can lead to critical losses of concentration and continuity.

COMPETITION

Compulsive zealots! The competition has nothing better to do than to do better. It has nothing more to live for than being the BEST. It is untroubled by the troubling, undaunted by the impossible, only strengthened by adversity, and absolutely inexhaustable. We can stand toe-to-toe with it, get out of the way, or get run over.

"Altitude is not gained by 'cruising'."

*****

"Even to <u>glide</u>, one has to climb to a significant height and leap into a void against a head-wind."

*****

"One must know what is <u>expected</u>; understand what is <u>required</u>; be prepared to invest the necessary <u>principle</u> and <u>interest</u>; and commit to paying the <u>full fare</u>."

*****

CHALLENGES OF THE <u>WORST</u> KIND

<u>WANTON WILLFULNESS</u>

We'd really rather <u>not</u> do lots of things that <u>need</u> doing — particularly if somebody ELSE wants or needs them done! MØst ⊚F τHe ⊥imΣ, ʊe'Я E doIng gReαt JʊSt to m∀nàG∃ S a 𝒩i T Y !! Should recourse finally run out — and, maybe, if we FEEL like it — we'll go ahead and suffer through it. But we reserve for ourselves the inalienable right to do OUR OWN THING, OUR OWN WAY on OUR OWN TERMS.

<u>SHORT-SIGHTEDNESS</u>

We often fail to connect the desired ultimate goal with the required investment. The instant "fix" is always most "expedient", immediate gratification commands "first sovereignty", and "pressing" is defined as what should have been done <u>yesterday</u>.

<u>THE SHORT CIRCUIT</u>

No matter how "cut and dried" a project or process may seem, a <u>methodical approach</u> and <u>strategic planning</u> can be critical to its success. When time is short, this central part of the process may be sacrificed or overlooked altogether, normal checks and balances are not engaged, and the ensuing "short circuit" fails to give the desired result.

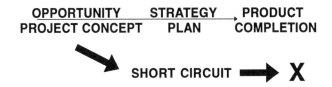

OPPORTUNITY	STRATEGY	PRODUCT
PROJECT CONCEPT	PLAN	COMPLETION

SHORT CIRCUIT ➡ X

<u>APATHY</u>

Not to CARE is the greatest tragedy.

"We have come to believe that the key success factor in business is simply getting one's arms around almost any practical problem and knocking it off — now."

Thomas J. Peters and
       Robert H. Waterman, Jr. [2]

"The only imaginable goal which cannot be achieved is that for which TIME has run out."

*****

BASIC TOIT

The BASIC TOIT is the simplest embodiment of key ingredients necessary to move forward. Somewhere between the knee-jerk reaction and CYA paralysis lies the need to "get a handle" on the challenge before us, establish the appropriate goal, put the plan in place for its completion, energize it, and move it on ahead — WHATEVER IT TAKES — BEGINNING NOW! The BASIC TOIT directs our attention toward that which is most IMPORTANT, most POSSIBLE and most NECESSARY — i.e., most BASIC — for ultimate progress.

*****

EXTENDED SYMBOL REPRESENTATIONS

Curiously embedded within the BASIC TOIT symbol — also frontwards, backwards and upside down — are several other important symbolic letters and acronyms. These include:

I ("I am CENTRAL TOIT and totally responsible");

IO ("I owe [those who came before me, those who stand beside me, those who will follow me—and MYSELF] my best effort");

C ("Commit, Concentrate, Check/Double Check, Confirm, Connect, Cope, and CHARGE .... C<>Z the moment!");

DOIT ("Don't Only Imagine...TRY!")
"Don't Only Initate...TERMINATE!").

Finally, the reclining letter "H" is a subtle reminder to "Hustle", "Be Helpful", "Maintain Honor" and "Cultivate HABITS of Excellence" (Stephen Covey, ref. 31).

"Every man takes the limits of his own field of vision for the limits of the world."

Arthur Schopenhauer [3]

PERSPECTIVE TOIT

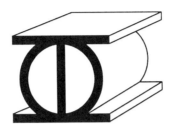

THINGS MUST BE KEPT IN PROPER PERSPECTIVE!*

Every worthy cause or project needs a willing buyer.
DON'T FORGET WHO'S BUYING!

Consider the multiple dimensions of the process or project at hand. It is important to leave ample room for the unorthodox approach; a quarter- to half-turn of the kaleidoscope can change possibilities instantly and immeasurably. Don't accept dogma or dicta unchallenged, nor rule them "void" out-of-hand.

The first/next item on the agenda is not necessarily the most important, nor is the first/next idea the most brilliant. DO-DO "reflex" actions often lead to "DOO-DOO" results. "First thoughts" share the same rights of first failure as of first fruits.

NOTE: TEST-TEST-TEST for proper depth, length and scale. Test the concept, a prototype, the "water", etc., but TEST-TEST-TEST! Perspective will often come more quickly —and always more accurately— from testing than from conjecture or consultation.

Finally, but certainly not least of all, add a HUMAN PERSPECTIVE TOIT. Along with the economic "bottom line" is a cost/benefit ratio in human terms. Both the end result and the process of getting there should include net positive contributions to personal dignity and an improvement of the human condition.

*TAKING CARE THAT IT DOESN'T LEAD TO
PARALYSIS!

9

"If it is to be, it is up to <u>me</u>."
Attributed to Denis Waitley [4]

ROUND TOIT

The ROUND TOIT is the most frequently "conjured" TOIT because it is the one with which we have the most consistent difficulty; i.e., overcoming inertia to get a project off the launch pad.

A sign on a local church billboard proclaimed: "You never get ANYWHERE until you begin!" The ROUND TOIT is a reminder of this intractable fact of life.

But the ROUND TOIT has a second and equally important function; i.e., in dealing with matters so unfamiliar, unpleasant, formidable or difficult to handle that they are not easily or directly approachable. To gain ANY progress at all under these circumstances, we may have to WORK A ROUND TOIT from a variety of angles until we find an appropriate "handle", an open door or a workable lock and key combination, or until we simply "wear it down-to-size".

CAUTION: The indirect approach can become so tangential that it may miss the mark entirely. It is quite fortuitous that the ROUND TOIT symbol carries a built-in "Bull's Eye" to help keep the TARGET of our efforts in plain view.

11

"We expect <u>absolute</u> dedication and perfection in performance of our sports and entertainment figures. We (THEY) should expect no less of ourselves."

*****

Put Your MIND TOIT

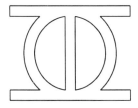

A serious mental commitment is an obligatory first step in "finally getting around to it". One must SOMEHOW, and AT SOME POINT, come to terms with the absolute certainty that the project

      IS WORTH DOING
      CAN be done
      HAS to be done
      is GOING TO BE DONE
      will be given PRIORITY, etc.

The required commitment may have <u>vast</u> ramifications: TOTAL commitment at SOME time and for SOME period will be necessary. Having "half-a-mind" to do it with only half-vast intentions guarantees that it will more than "half" to be done over with exponentially greater investment.

     *   *   *   *   *

SYMBOL REPRESENTATION NOTE:

As pointed out in the PREFACE, the "open" (i.e., unfilled) TOIT symbol is used throughout the manuscript as a generic representation of important TOIT concepts which do not have easily recognizable symbolic renderings. It is particularly fitting that the <u>initial</u> open symbol of the TOIT series represents this particular concept —"Put Your MIND TOIT"— for we must strive to keep a CLEAR and OPEN MIND in all that we do! The axiomatic first corollary of this principle is simply:

             "BE OPEN TOIT".

"I do not believe in a fate that falls on men however they act; but I do believe in a fate that falls on men UNLESS they act."

Gilbert K. Chesterton [5]

UP TOIT
WORK UP TOIT
GEAR UP TOIT
GET UP TOIT
FEEL UP TOIT

Hatchling enterprises require incubation, inspiration, strategic planning, nurturing, sifting, sorting, prioritization, orientation, preparation, training, information gathering, nudging, timing/scheduling, etc. The more groundwork invested, the smoother the road to implementation. This effort should be started well ahead of schedule, even sandwiching between other priorities where possible, so that everything is ready to go — and thoroughly UP TOIT (including YOU) — when it's time to hit the deck running.

NOTE 1: It is not out-of-bounds to invoke assistance from all relevant other resource bases in managing to get one's self UP TOIT.

NOTE 2:

When you don't 'feel' like it, do it anyway!

"A man who has to be convinced to act before he acts is not a man of action...you must act as you breathe."

Georges Clemenceau [5]

DOWN TOIT

Getting seriously <u>down-to-business</u> can be a ponderous undertaking. One risks the fatal illusion that <u>thinking about it</u> is the same as actually <u>working on it</u>. Although the "wheels" may be "turning" at the highest possible rates, nothing will move an iota unless the gears become engaged and the "rubber hits the road". GETTING DOWN TOIT must be a process in earnest — fully engaged — once the determination has been made to proceed.

"Pounds are the sons not of pounds, but of pence."

Charles Buxton [6]

"Method goes far to prevent Trouble in Business: For it makes the Task easy, hinders Confusion, [and] saves abundance of Time..."

William Penn [7]

SCALE DOWN TOIT
SCALE UP TOIT

No matter how grandiose a plan or a project, its substance must take shape one building block at a time from some elemental beginning and it must be simplified to the most manageable components/stages of progress. The important thing is to begin somewhere...sometimes <u>anywhere</u> will do. The virtue of a first draft, "first thoughts" or a prototype cannot be underestimated in simply getting the project off the ground. <u>Neither can the smallest detail be ignored</u>.

Once started, firmly within grasp, proven worthy and targeted to the right end-point, SCALING UP begins; "fleshing it out", setting benchmarks for production, lining up all resources and services to be invoked, etc.

METHOD TOIT

Develop a WORKABLE plan — and follow it!

19

"No distance is ever so far as a turn in the wrong direction."

*****

STRAIGHT TOIT

Peripheral issues/concerns and trivial pursuits be damned!

Cut out the nonsense.

Confront it head-on

and

GET STRAIGHT TOIT!

"Nothing in the World can take the place of persistence. Talent will not; nothing is more common than unsuccessful men with talent. Genius will not; unrewarded genius is almost a proverb. Education will not; the world is full of educated derelicts. Persistence and determination are omnipotent. The slogan "press on" has solved and always will solve the problems of the human race."

Attributed to Calvin Coolidge
(unverified) [8]

STICK TOIT
HOLD ON TOIT

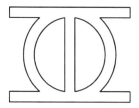

Whatever the objective, one must develop the conviction that it is not only worth DOING, but worth FINISHING — and WITH CLASS.

Detachment and indifference are fatal and distraction isn't worth the trouble it will cause. Likewise, the short-cut toward getting it done faster or cheaper or toward getting on with another priority will only lead to disappointment.

<u>Be uncompromising</u>!

STICK TOIT!
and
HOLD ON TOIT

until it is deservedly finished!!

NOTE: Where mental or physical exhaustion threaten, or when a project seems to have gotten hopelessly bogged down, reach into whatever reserve you can muster and take a SECOND INITIATIVE. Pace yourself, take smaller steps and engage all other help necessary to "break out of the rut". TAKE CHARGE anew and STICK TOIT!

"Incubation has intrinsic merit —
but it has to be started early and
needs tending. Any process left
entirely to the good graces of
MOTHER NATURE, THE
ALMIGHTY, or THERMO-
DYNAMIC EQUILIBRATION will
be a determinedly untargeted
process — for all <u>practical</u>
purposes."

*****

GET BACK TOIT

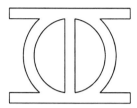

Any number of pressing exigencies may reach a stage of importance critical enough to move a key project aside, even if ever so temporarily. Particularly during the incubation period, a project is easily lost in the midst of other pursuits. Such infringements <u>usually</u> occur at the most <u>inopportune</u> times.

Where STICKING TOIT and/or HOLDING ON TOIT can not be managed, or where they would be inappropriate due to the intrinsic need for "simmering" or the sheer force of necessity, GETTING BACK TOIT is the one stop-gap safety valve for continuing to make progress.

"Success demands more than a good idea. It demands fanatical devotion."

Mortimer Levitt [9]

BUY-IN TOIT
COMMIT TOIT

Once a project "passes muster", be prepared to put <u>ALL</u> your resources into it: Time, effort, dollars ("buying power"/"chips", etc.), and reputation. Eat, sleep, drink, shave and shower with it. The extent to which you "buy in" will directly influence the actions of critical other investors. Let there be no question about your commitment. Remember, the person you most don't want to "fool" is <u>YOU</u>! Don't expect anyone else to take up the charge or challenge until you've ABSOLUTELY sold yourself.

"Life in business, as otherwise, is fundamentally a matter of attention — how we spend our time."

Thomas J. Peters and
        Robert H. Waterman, Jr. [10]

TEND TOIT
ATTEND TOIT

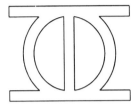

BE THERE! Don't be an absentee manager, no matter how much delegation may seem in order. Cultivate the enterprise, its leaders at the top and its troops at the front-line. Reach out and touch it and give it "hands on" attention. Let it become an integral part of your world. Don't just "sprinkle" it with water, give it some real substance to "grow" on, "prune" and "shape" it, and be a fanatic about the "weeds". Walk through every step of development and production. Wear parenthood graciously and responsibly. Don't let it become an orphan.

TEND TOIT!

"Recently, TI...found that one factor marked EVERY failure: 'Without exception we found we hadn't had a VOLUNTEER champion.'"

Thomas J. Peters and
     Robert H. Waterman, Jr.
          (quoting a TI executive) [11]

"If men could regard the events of their lives with more open minds, they would frequently discover that they did not really desire the thing they failed to obtain."

André Maurois [12]

Put Your
Whole HEART
in TOIT

A project well done requires a whole heart, along with the requisite amounts of soul and mind and strength. If your heart's not in it, it isn't going to go very far or do very well. A job or project worth doing is worth doing with ALL the heart you can muster. (Even if it's not a "missionary" project, somebody's got to LOVE it a little.)

"The first loss is usually the smallest loss — take it and run."

Business Axiom

OWN UP TOIT

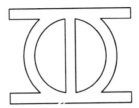

Take credit where credit is due—and OWN UP TOIT when it falls short (or exceeds the credit line)!

Nothing goes awry in a vacuum; the redeeming feature of a mistake is that somebody <u>dared enough to try</u>!

The band director's admonition was "Make your mistake loud enough so we can fix it".

If it needs doing, take the risk* and OWN UP TOIT if it doesn't work out.

GROUND RULES:

1. The need or desired benefit must be worth the risk.
2. The risk must have noble intent.
3. There must be enough "chips" in escrow to pay the piper.**

* The earlier, the better.

** Impeccable integrity is TRUMP in all circumstances.
   Make it your highest priority - no excuses.

"You never compromise UP."
Gilbert H. Friedell, M.D. [13]

" 'ENOUGH' is when you can't do any MORE"

*****

"To provide the extra margin of merit is to do that which—for all 'practical' purposes—is 'UNNECESSARY' ."

*****

Put QUALITY IN TOIT

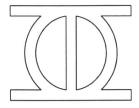

Don't just finish it with a strip of chrome on the outside or a "look" of butter in the frosting; give it a fighting chance in the universal marketplace full of skeptics and brutal competition. Remember: Whatever you leave behind stands in your place. Do yourself justice!

NOT ONLY, BUT ALSO...AND (NOBA) TOIT

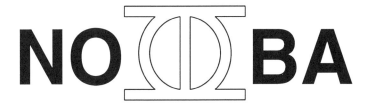

PREMISE: There is often <u>at least</u> ONE MORE THING we can do to improve outcome. Some things added will enhance and some will detract—and it is essential to know the difference. But we must not simply meet <u>minimum</u> standards and expectations: Our paper carrier <u>NOT ONLY</u> gets our paper delivered by 6 a.m., <u>**BUT ALSO**</u> wraps it in plastic on rainy days <u>AND</u> puts it right beside our front door!
<u>NOBA does it better!</u>

NOTE: The NOBA TOIT is the only TOIT in this series to be represented by an acronym without natural occurrence in everyday conversation. Its contribution to TRUE QUALITY, however, is inestimable.

"In going where you have to go, and doing what you have to do, and seeing what you have to see, you dull and blunt the instrument you write with. But I would rather have it bent and dull and know I had to put it on the grindstone again and hammer it into shape and put a whetstone to it, and know that I had something to write about, than to have it bright and shining and nothing to say, or smooth and well-oiled in the closet, but unused."

Ernest Hemingway [14]

PUT HEAT TOIT

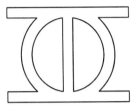

Often we can get so involved in just bringing a project to feasibility or functionality — perhaps having set our sights only to that point — that we fall short of gaining its true potential. It is important to press on, "nudging" it along from every direction to make sure it "holds water", "stands up to the heat" and "delivers the goods". Final steps should include efforts to refine, temper, braze, "hone", sand and polish it to perfection.

Then ask for a second opinion!

NOTE: It is amazing what an interim evaluation will do: At each benchmark consider where you could have taken the project if you had had the privilege of <u>starting</u> where you are now.

"In the fields of observation, chance favors only the prepared mind."

Inaugural Lecture
University of Lille
December 7, 1854
Louis Pasteur [15]

IN TOIT
INTUIT

Put everything you've got IN TOIT and watch the INTUIT take over! The "obvious" is only obvious to the <u>prepared</u> <u>mind</u>. Getting IN TOIT — hook, line and sinker — prepares the way for the OBVIOUS to happen, as though driven by INTUIT-ION.

"My green thumb came only as a result of the mistakes I made while learning to see things from the plant's point of view."

H. Fred Ale [16]

"Those who keep coming out on top have the habit of working at things with missionary zeal — with nothing plausibly 'better' to do."

*****

LOOK IN TOIT

Go into a project "with your eyes open". Do the appropriate research. Look at it through other people's eyes. Envision its true potential and final manifestation. "Walk" through it in your mind until you begin to see it materialize in every detail.

SEE TOIT

If not now.....WHY NOT?

If not now.....WHEN?

If not you.....WHO?

If not HIS/HER/THEIR way.....HOW?

Put on all the qualifications you want;

Fuss and fume all the way to the finish line if you MUST;

but
SEE TO IT **ANYWAY!**

"There is value in disaster. All our mistakes are burned up. Now we can start anew."

Thomas Edison [17]

(On sifting through the ashes after his entire company had gone up in flames.)

GIVE IN TOIT

The GIVE IN TOIT has two important dimensions. First, there a distinct virtue in understanding your limitations and in knowing when to quit and start over, or use a new "tack" (i.e., if at first you don't succeed, try another method!) Second, it is important to recognize the fact that a matter may need to be dealt with on its own terms, not necessarily on terms prescribed arbitrarily or dogmatically by the manager or greater organization. Management by sheer force or decree may create both the proverbial "rock" and "a hard place" between which one may, unfortunately, get stuck at some inopportune point in the future.

NOTE: "Giving IN" is NOT "Giving UP"!

CONCEDE TOIT

The strategic concession can sometimes be one of the most powerful "currencies" in progress. (Don't underestimate the value of concessions already given or of accumulated I.O.U.'s.) A strategic retreat can often buy time, allow the consolidation of 'armaments', and change the field of battle to a remarkable advantage.

Conversely, an absolute resolve toward winning all points can be an absolute absurdity, even if it's absolutely justified. Being DEAD RIGHT can result in being just as DEAD as RIGHT!

NOTE 1: You can't lose what was not yours in the beginning.

NOTE 2: Not for concession are COMMON SENSE, DECENCY, INTEGRITY, VISION, PERSPECTIVE and a SENSE OF HUMOR.

"...as with the storm-tossed ship, that miserably drives along the leeward land...With all her might she crowds all sail off shore... 'gainst the very winds that fain would blow her homeward...for refuge's sake forlornly rushing into peril; her only friend her bitterest foe!"

Herman Melville [18]

SUBJECT(ed) TOIT

A project and its manager can become SUBJECTed to many opposing forces and priorities, being pushed and pulled in so many different directions that the odds against success become overwhelming. A good project and a good manager, however, will survive the odds and perhaps even emerge enriched. To succeed under such circumstances, it may be necessary to "roll with the punches" — where appropriate — and stand up to the heat when necessary.

The SUBJECT(ed) TOIT is a reminder that the course of events is not always easy, but that, by facing it square on and persisting, one will more likely survive, and, eventually, conquer.

"If it weren't for the last minute, nothing would ever get done."

Anonymous

"One need only remember our horror when the space shuttle Challenger Exploded. When everything goes smoothly, we tend to relax our vigil. It is human nature."

W. French Anderson [19]

"The time for taking all measures for a ship's safety is while still able to do so."

Admiral Nimitz in a letter
to the Pacific Fleet
18 February 1945 [20]

It is easy to overlook — and/or get overrun by — the 11TH HOUR CHALLENGE: Major projects will <u>only</u> get done the <u>right</u> way at the <u>right</u> time by investing a proportionate amount of 11th hour overtime. Delay is an absolute certainty. First, the required incubation time, routine matters-of-course and interruptions will offset even the most conservative deadline projections. Second, one invariably suffers from "light at the end of the tunnel" syndrome: The more light coming in, the more visible are all of the hurdles yet to overcome. Finally, the search for perfection is never complete.

One should be well prepared for the 11TH HOUR CHALLENGE and incorporate it into the overall plan from the beginning.

Have your crisis early!

"Too often, our minds are locked on one track. We are looking for red — so we overlook blue. Many Nobel Prizes have been washed down the drain because someone did not expect the unexpected."

John D. Turner [21]

UN-TOIT

The UN-TOIT is an inside out TOIT. This symbol and concept represent the need to turn a project "inside out" to determine — but not tamper with — those qualities and characteristics that are innate, unique and/or essential UNTO IT. Every effort should be made to enhance those characteristics; like Michelangelo, we should attempt to "set free" the true essence of what lies hidden within the project (UNknown or UNrealized) and bring it to life.

NOTE: This process will also reveal any hidden "land mines" capable of bringing the project and its participants to an untimely demise!

"Power is not revealed by striking hard or often but by striking true."

Honoré de Balzac [22]

CENTRAL TOIT

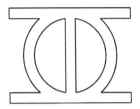

As we have already seen, surrounding circumstances can dramatically affect outcome. Things political, personal and otherwise peripheral can overwhelm OR enhance a project. A focus on matters most CENTRAL TOIT is imperative. An astute manager may even need to isolate him or herself and the mission at hand from impinging factors in order for proper FOCUS to be maintained. As important as it is to "set the stage", "build bridges", "clear the rafters", and "rig the atmosphere" to create just the right environ/mental conditioning, it is essential to avoid preoccupation in these areas — any one of which might legitimately be invoked as critical to the overall project. Emphasis on those things most CENTRAL TOIT will breed the most success.

<u>Stick to the HEART of the matter with fanatic conviction and don't let it out of your sight</u>!

"The sky may be the limit, but unless you hitch your wagon to more than a remote twinkle, you risk getting lost in the void or being swept into a black hole."

*****

LINK TOIT

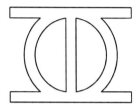

Anything kept to itself in the face of a revolution in systems integration will lose valuable reinforcement and "leverageability".

Discover and apply the virtues of synergy between projects and other resources wherever they can be found.

"It is the mark of a good action that it appears inevitable in retrospect."

Robert Louis Stevenson [23]

NOTHING TOIT

....
. . .
.   .   .
.   .   .
.   .   .
. . .
....

The NOTHING TOIT is one of the most deceptive TOITs. Something of value does not come from nothing. Accomplishments that appear to require "no sweat" actually benefit from hidden endowments: The requisite TOOLS and EXPERIENCE.

The NOTHING TOIT is also important in underlining the fact that we occasionally make "mountains out of molehills", imagining all sorts of "somethings" unassailable and generating a paralysis of the "great unknown". The unknown is usually threatening only because it is unfamiliar. Knowledge (EXPERIENCE) and craftsmanship (having the right TOOLS and knowing how to use them) will dispel the unfounded mountain of concern to show that there is NOTHING TOIT!

"Sometimes when I consider what tremendous consequences come from little things...I am tempted to think...there are no little things."

Bruce Barton [24]

"Fewer people have been criticized for taking total responsibility than for taking total credit."

*****

"Often the only REAL progress we make is that engendered by GOING OUT OF OUR WAY."

*****

"Commit thoughtless acts of necessity."

*****

Most of us have no problem attacking the major challenges of life: Slaying dragons, climbing Mt. Everest, or coursing along interstates in 4,000 pound missiles at 80 miles per hour. More often it's the minor things with which we have greatest difficulty and which, left undone, take the real "stuffing" out of life ... the supplies that didn't get replaced, the phone call not made, the conference room that nobody got ready, the "O" ring that's missing, etc. ...

Some matters require SIMPLE BRUTE FORCE: They can not be ignored; they can not be delegated — due to time, skill or circumstance; they can not be fabricated from existing resources by cut-and-paste; they can not be managed by remote control; and they can not be moved by invocation of the Almighty, however sincere.

> Try putting a PENCIL to PAPER when the computer goes down!

STOOP TOIT!   Take a deep breath, grasp a full measure of intimate responsibility, roll up the sleeves of your most heavily stuffed shirt, and JUST DO IT! Reserve for yourself sufficient <u>pride of ownership</u>, <u>flexibility</u>, and <u>fortitude</u> that you may never be so elevated, arthritic or out-of-touch that you cannot STOOP to deal with matters DIRECTLY—on whatever terms necessary to get the job done.

He who leads best leads by example and commands; he does not ask of others that which he would not himself stoop to do if and when circumstances require it, no matter WHO the job "belongs to".

> If it's <u>EVERYBODY'S</u> responsibility,
> don't let <u>NOBODY</u> do it.

> IF IT NEEDS DOING NOW,
> NO MATTER HOW FAR "BENEATH" YOU IT IS,
> <u>DO IT</u>!

"We must walk consciously only part way toward our goal, and then leap in the dark to our success."

Attributed to
    Henry David Thoreau,
        (unverified) [25]

"We need people who are impatient — who will push the limits of entrenched practice and authority, insofar as possible or necessary — to achieve new levels of understanding and accomplishment."

*****

GO TOIT
GET TOIT
HOP TOIT
WADE IN TOIT
DIVE IN TOIT
TEAR IN TOIT

When it's finally time for action, GO TOIT! WADE IN where it's new and uncharted, DIVE IN where it's familiar or fathomable, and SLOG THROUGH IT when the going gets tough. But when the time comes, GO TOIT and give it everything you've got!

*"If we make conscious boundaries —
outlining what we <u>will</u> and <u>will not</u>
do, and WHEN we will or will not
do it — we must be prepared to live
within those boundaries and not
begrudge those who 'laid it all on
the line' their success."*

*****

*"Taking time is a thief's trade;
making time a strategist's. An
effective manager must be both
strategist and thief, stealing time
from less compelling or more
leisurely pursuits to get the job
done."*

*****

CAVEAT:
TOIT SUBVERSIONS

As noted throughout this work, effective applications of the major TOITs may actually have less to do with elements of the project at hand than with myriad other factors, many of which may be of significantly lower priority. Ironically, such other factors may be sufficiently inconsequential in substance as to <u>seem</u> inconsequential in effect, when, in fact, they may directly or indirectly — separately or collectively — cause major interference, draining essential TIME and ENERGY by imperceptibly small steps.

<u>TIME</u> and <u>ENERGY</u> are critical TOIT elements. It is important to make these elements COUNT! The costs of "shooting the breeze", speculating on the ethereal, complaining to persons who are not in positions to fix things, indulging the latest gossip, preparing a "brief" on something you may use "someday", lingering over the mail or a phone call, or being generally "sociable", in short, tending the ever present distractions of the workplace, are inestimable.

Many successful managers have learned how to subvert the subversions by relegating them to their own time slots where they can compete against each other rather than against major projects and priorities.

An equally significant, and all too frequent, TOIT subversion factor is the **"DREAD KNOT"**: the dreaded phone call, meeting or other activity which, in its foreboding, can tie you, your intestinal fortitude and all extant projects and activities into an intractable paralysis. The DREAD KNOT can exhaust the very resources one can be in desperate need to conserve. Whatever the cause, "frame" it: Put it on stop-motion, tie it down, run a "scouting mission", throw up a trial balloon, formulate a strategy of approach, then grit your teeth and go do it—the sooner, the better. DO NOT LET IT SETTLE FOR ONE MOMENT UNTIL THERE IS NOTHING MORE TO SETTLE!

"He has called on the best that was in us... We might not be the best, and none of us were, but we were to make the effort to be the best. 'After you have done the best you can,' he used to say, 'the hell with it.'"

Senator Robert F. Kennedy,
     tribute to his father,
        Joseph P. Kennedy.
Read at Joseph Kennedy's funeral
     by Senator Edward M. Kennedy
         November 20, 1969 [26]

"No comment."

Doug Moe, on hearing that he
     had been voted the most
         quotable coach in the National
            Basketball Association [27]

NO END TOIT
(PUT A) STOP TOIT

Finally! ENOUGH IS ENOUGH!!*

Things peripheral can tend to drag on to the point of becoming not only perpetual annoyances but, in the extreme case, insufferable millstones. When something has reached — or threatens to break through — the most illogical conclusion to which it can be indulged, it is more than half-past time to PUT A STOP TOIT!

NOTE: PUTTING A STOP TOIT will often require much more creativity than either GEARING UP TOIT or GETTING DOWN TOIT.

*NO MORE TOITs, ALREADY!

"But above all try something."

FDR [28]

"Somebody said that it
    couldn't be done
But he with a chuckle replied
    That 'maybe it couldn't'
but he would be one
    who wouldn't say so
        till he tried.

So he buckled right in
    with a trace of a grin
If he worried he hid it.
He started to sing
    as he tackled the thing
That couldn't be done
    and he did it."

Edgar A. Guest [29]

A TOIT TALE

The atmosphere at the Annual Meeting was filled with electric anticipation: A rumored "top secret" project was about to be unveiled and few had any CLUE TOIT. Speculation had attached military OVERTONES TOIT, but "insiders" claimed there was no TRUTH TOIT.

The Board was confident that the entire work force would SUBSCRIBE TOIT. Consultants were on hand to lend CREDIBILITY TOIT. Management was unquestionably COMMITTED TOIT. Those on furlough certainly looked FORWARD TOIT. Nonetheless, "Vaporware Veterans" doubted that there would be much SUBSTANCE TOIT.

Formal presentation was accomplished with great FANFARE TOIT. The CEO beamed with pride during the INTRODUCTION TOIT. The chief architect gave critical DETAIL and DEFINITION TOIT. The Chairman of the Board added important DIMENSIONS TOIT. Anyone could see that the design team had put a lot of THOUGHT TOIT. Innovation analysts were delighted to find many features UNIQUE TOIT. Business analysts saw distinct ADVANTAGES TOIT. An almost supernatural phenomenology was ASCRIBED TOIT. **And to think they had really only <u>BACKED IN TOIT</u>!**

A marketing team was immediately ASSIGNED TOIT. They had not seen anything SIMILAR TOIT. Distributers lined up to CHECK IN TOIT. Competitors tried in vain to conceive of possible DETERRENTS TOIT; but even those most adamant were ultimately RESIGNED TOIT. Consumers made immediate ADJUSTMENTS TOIT. Still, a few cautious investors had trouble GETTING USED TOIT.

In the end, there was little that anyone could recall COMPARED TOIT. It had made its mark and was here to stay— <u>and that's ALL THERE WAS TOIT</u>!

*"Don't just stand there -
    INVENT!"*

Inscription over the entrance to
    the Public Search Room at the
        Patent and Trademark Office,
        Washington, DC

*"Do <u>SOMETHING</u> about
<u>SOMETHING</u> . . .
    GET **TOIT**
    and
MAKE A DIFFERENCE."*

*****

MISCELLANEOUS TOITs

The listing of TOITs has no discernable end! Below is a compilation of TOITs (in more or less random order) which appeared in various settings during the course of finalizing this manual. These miscellaneous TOITs have not yet been endowed with annotations. Many are similar to TOITs already noted, a number are obvious and don't require annotation, and others simply don't justify it. They are provided here for general reference. Use this list as a beginning for your own compendium of TOITs and see how far you can go!

SOMETHING TOIT	ADAPT TOIT
PRIORITY TOIT	RISK TOIT
MORE TOIT (than meets the eye)	SENSE TOIT
(Give) RECOGNITION TOIT	BEHOLDEN TOIT
(Pay) ATTENTION TOIT	AMENABLE TOIT
(Add) DISTINCTION TOIT	REACTION TOIT
(Get/Don't get) MARRIED TOIT	LIMIT TOIT
TWO SIDES TOIT	ASSENT TOIT
VALIDITY TOIT	STAND UP TOIT
ASPIRE TOIT	SWEAR TOIT
LAY CLAIM TOIT	CHECK-IN TOIT
ACCEDE TOIT	AKIN TOIT
(Pay) HOMAGE TOIT	DUE TOIT
AVERSION TOIT	ADAPT TOIT
GROW IN TOIT	ADD TOIT
LISTEN TOIT	LICENSE TOIT
SUBSCRIBE TOIT	TITLE TOIT
(Don't) SURRENDER TOIT	NO POINT TOIT
(Be) SENSITIVE TOIT	SHAPE TOIT
(Be) RECEPTIVE TOIT	SIMILAR TOIT
RESPOND TOIT	CLOSE TOIT
ADVANTAGE TOIT	APPROACH TOIT
(Come) HOME TOIT	COME TOIT
RESPITE TOIT	ADJACENT TOIT
(Put some) MUSCLE TOIT	NEXT TOIT
CONDEMNED TOIT	SEQUEL TOIT

"I am miserly with my time in some areas so that I can be profligate with it in others."

Stanley Marcus [30]

"Once you realize what it really takes — that life's tough and nothing really worthwhile comes without all the effort you've got — it's a piece of cake!"

*****

PERSONAL NOTE

The WANT and NEED to achieve are basic to the "human condition", but they often exceed the endowed DRIVE. To compound matters, what "drive" one CAN muster is largely consumed by limitless day-to-day challenges just to "keep even". Unfortunately, we often respond by adjusting our goals downward to fill in the gap. TOITs are intended to help narrow the gap, hold us "even", and keep us on course.

But TOITs are not only reminders to <u>work harder</u>. No power plant can sustain peak output without constant replenishment of the raw materials that drive it and without proper maintenance of its infrastructure. Peak output in "person power" is no different. We must maintain adequate physical, mental, spiritual and "psychic" reserves — and in proper balance — to achieve our highest goals. TOITs are conduits to help us <u>work smarter</u> and <u>live more intentionally</u>. While at times we are engaged by ABSOLUTE IMPERATIVES to STAND AND DELIVER the SUPREME GOODS — no apologies/no excuses, the wholesale sacrifice of human sensitivity and sensibility is an unforgiving loss. "People" resources, including a whole YOU, are the real bricks and mortar in the road to success and they need to be maintained in peak condition.

The fundamental TOIT message is:

> When you work, work as you've never worked before, but don't stop there; seize all of the rest of life that your numbered minutes and hours can offer. Plan and prioritize and develop habits which will make ALL you do much more effective, including essential "housekeeping", service, leisure, self-renewal and self-realization activities.

Whatever people on their death beds ultimately confess, the most common retrospective lament is: "I wish I had taken more time...."

TAKING time and MAKING time for PRIORITY ENDEAVORS, which include renewal activities, undergird <u>all</u> TOIT principles.

69

"The key is not to prioritize your schedule but to schedule your priorities."

Stephen R. Covey [31]

FINAL NOTE

First attempts to apply TOIT principles are accompanied by the tendency to place EVERYTHING on the list of "things to do" at number 1 priority. This tendency can lead to intractable stress and eventual "burn out". Prioritization, done correctly, is neither strictly a vertical or a horizontal ranking exercise but a time/value-weighted dynamic process. The critical elements in prioritization are careful assessments of WHAT HAS TO BE DONE, WHAT CAN BE DISCHARGED WITH DISPATCH, WHAT CAN BE STARTED NOW AND PLACED IN MOTION, and WHAT CAN BE SCHEDULED AT A LATER TIME (as long as its own priority time is actually scheduled). Often the hardest choice for a "can do" person is what not to do NOW, and what not to do ALTOGETHER.

SECRETS
OF
"UNLIKELY"
CHAMPIONS

*They have nothing <u>BETTER</u> to do
than TO DO THEIR BEST;
They have NOTHING TO LOSE
except that which they do not
want to become;
They have nothing MORE
IMPORTANT to hang onto
than the FUTURE; and
They have NOWHERE TO GO
BUT <u>UP</u>.
Their success comes not from
stunning beauty, family name,
personal "connections" or
social grace,
But from sheer force of will and
applied determination.*

*****

POSTSCRIPT 1

The most unfortunate challenges of life not explicitly mentioned in the primary text are UNFAIRNESS and DISCRIMINATION. We must recognize that these unconscionable forces DO exist and we must do everything possible to eliminate them and minimize their impact wherever they occur.

POSTSCRIPT 2

The following TOITs were purposely not included in this work:

    (I'm) ENTITLED TOIT
    (I've Gotta) RIGHT TOIT
    (I'm) IMMUNE TOIT.

It is this author's conviction that "entitlements", "rights", "privileges" and "immunities" are much too liberally acclaimed and frequently extended beyond all reasonable proportion. For the most part, the great job you did today "entitles" you to come back and do the same — or greater — job tomorrow. That grand family name, company position, etc., gives you the "right" to behave in such a way as to validate its nobility and enhance the stature it had when it was given to you.

"...fill the unforgiving minute with sixty seconds worth of distance run..."

Rudyard Kipling [32]

"Success is never having to say:

'I could have done better...'
'If I only had
one more chance...'
'I simply ran out of time...'
'It wasn't <u>my</u> fault!' "

*****

APPENDIX

"Every action — and every inaction — is either an INVESTMENT or an EXPENDITURE. It is the <u>combined portfolio</u> of investments and expenditures, together with the STANDARDS and VALUES against which they are measured, that determines the true 'bottom line' of success."

*****

"Success is having the CAPACITY and INCLINATION to contribute."

*****

WHAT DOES "OWNING" A TOIT MEAN?

"Owning" a TOIT means <u>taking ultimate responsibility for your life</u>. It means consistently focusing on matters that count — matters that make a difference — in your work, your family, your community, and all other aspects of your life.

Your responsibility in "owning" a TOIT is to make the most of available TIME and ENERGY to improve yourself and your effectiveness in all that you do. It means being INTENTIONAL and not letting life just "happen". It means:

> --Taking <u>initiative</u>;
> --Anticipating problems and opportunities:
> --Staying "on task" to finish assignments;
> --Being resourceful;
> --Sacrificing indulgences;
> --Being accountable;
> --Doing it right the FIRST time.

It also means:

> --NOT having to "cut corners";
> --NOT having to make excuses;
> --NOT "lingering" over matters that don't count;
> --NOT settling for "half-a-loaf".

It means preparing for and taking on the challenges, picking up the gauntlet, and finishing it off — WITH EXCELLENCE — NOW!

"Owning" a TOIT is having a personal license to DO THE RIGHT THING and to say "NO" to all that will compromise the best you can be or do.

It is a talisman against all odds and a fortification against all challenges.

APPENDIX II

THE TOIT MEDALLION

Five CORE TOIT CONCEPTS are encapsulated in a 1.5 inch diameter TOIT medallion, schematically shown below.   The face side of the medallion incorporates the BASIC TOIT symbol and the reverse displays symbols of the four most active "working" TOITs:

> The ROUND TOIT
> The UP TOIT
> The DOWN TOIT, and
> The BUY-IN TOIT.

The medallion "reads" as follows:

> SIDE I: **"GET TOIT!"**   and   **"DOIT!"**
> "Take On Important Tasks!"
> "Take On Immediate Tasks"
> "Take On Imaginable Tasks"
> "I am centrally responsible"
> "IOwe my best effort"
> "Don't Only Imagine...TRY!"
> "Don't Only Initiate...TERMINATE!"
> "C<>Z the moment (Commit, Concentrate...CHARGE!)".
> "HUSTLE", "Be HELPFUL", "Maintain Honor"
> "Cultivate Habits of EXCELLENCE"

> SIDE II: "Besides first (FINALLY!)
>   GETTING AROUND TOIT,
>   One must consciously GEAR UP TOIT,
>   Get seriously DOWN TOIT,
>   And absolutely BUY-IN TOIT."

APPENDIX III

REFERENCES

1. Eisenhower, D.D., as quoted by James C. Humes in: PODIUM HUMOR: A Raconteur's Treasury of Witty and Humorous Stories. New York: Harper & Row, 1985; p. 184.

2. Peters, Thomas J., and Waterman, Robert H., Jr. In Search of Excellence. New York: Harper & Row, 1982; p. 126.

3. Schopenhauer, Arthur "Further Psychological Observations", in: Parerga and Paralipomena (1851) tr. T. Bailey Saunders, ref.: The International Thesaurus of Quotations. New York: Thomas Y. Crowell Company, 1970; p. 466.

4. Waitley, Denis, as quoted by L. Reed Polk in: Running into a DEADEND While Escaping. Lexington, KY: Lexington House, 1990; p. 20. Alternately attributed to William H. Johnson (ref. unverified).

5. As quoted by W.H. Alden and Louis Kronenberger in: The Viking Book of APHORISMS: A Personal Selection. New York: Dorset Press, 1988; p. 252.

6. Buxton, Charles, as quoted by Tryon Edwards, D.D., in: The New Dictionary of Thoughts: A Cyclopedia of Quotations (Revised and Enlarged by C.N. Catrevas, Jonathan Edwards, and Ralph Emerson Browns). New York: Standard Book Company, 1966; p. 645.

7. Penn, William "Some Fruits of Solitude" in: Reflections & Maxims, no. 403, p. 70 (1903, reprinted 1976). Referenced in: Respectfully Quoted: A Dictionary of Quotations Requested from the Congress Research Service (Suzy Platt, ed.). Washington: Library of Congress, 1989; p. 31.

8. Coolidge, Calvin, as recorded in: Respectfully Quoted: A Dictionary of Quotations Requested from the Congress Research Service (Suzy Platt, ed.). Washington: Library of Congress, 1989; p. 255.

9. Levitt, Mortimer How to Start Your Own Business Without Losing Your Shirt: Secrets of Seventeen Successful Entrepreneurs. New York: Harper & Row, 1982; p. 69.

10. Peters, Thomas J., and Waterman, Robert H., Jr. In Search of Excellence. New York: Harper & Row, 1982; p. 69.

11. Peters, Thomas J., and Waterman, Robert H., Jr. In Search of Excellence. New York: Harper & Row 1982; p. 203.

12. Maurois, André The Art of Living, as recorded in: The Wit and Wisdom of the 20th Century (compiled by Frank S. Pepper). New York: Peter Bedrick Books, 1987; p. 18 (#19).

13. Friedell, G.H., personal communication.

14. Hemingway, Ernest "Preface to the First Forty Nine" in: The Complete Short Stories of Ernest Hemingway: The Finca Vigia Edition. New York: Charles Scribner's Sons/Macmillan Publishing Company, 1987; p. 3.

15. Pasteur, Louis, as recorded in: Bartlett's Familiar Quotations (Sixteenth Edition). Boston: Little, Brown and Company, 1992; p. 502.

16. Ale, H. Fred, as quoted by Laurence J. Peter in: Peter's Quotations: Ideas for Our Time. New York: William Morrow and Company, 1977; p. 37.

17. Edison, Thomas, as quoted by Alan Loy McGinness in: The Power of Optimism. San Francisco: Harper-sanfrancisco, 1990, as referenced in: "Reader's Digest". Pleasantville, NY: Reader's Digest Association, Inc.; July 1991; p. 17.

18. Melville, Herman Moby Dick. New York: Random House, 1950, (Modern Library College Edition); p. 105.

19. Anderson, W. French "Reflections of Hope and Concern". Human Gene Therapy vol. 2 (no.3) Fall 1991; pp. 193-194.

20. Nimitz, Chester W., as cited in: Dictionary of Military and Naval Quotations. Heine, Col. R.D., Jr., USMC (Ret.), Annapolis, MD: 1966; p. 284.

21. Turner, John D., in: Textile Chemist & Colorist, as quoted by "Reader's Digest". Pleasantville, NY: Reader's Digest Association, Inc., October, 1991; p. 129.

22. Balzac, Honoré de, as quoted by W.H. Alden and Louis Kronenberger in: The Viking Book of APHORISMS: A Personal Selection. New York: Dorset Press, 1988; p. 246.

23. Stevenson, Robert Louis, as quoted by W.H. Alden and Louis Kronenberger in: <u>The Viking Book of APHORISMS: A Personal Selection</u>. New York: Dorset Press, 1988; p. 253.

24. Barton, Bruce, as quoted by Stephen Covey in: <u>The 7 Habits of Highly Effective People</u>. New York: Simon and Schuster, 1990; p. 287.

25. Referenced in: <u>Respectfully Quoted: A Dictionary of Quotations Requested from the Congress Research Service</u> (Suzy Platt, ed.). Washington: Library of Congress, 1989; p. 335, #1786.

26. Kennedy, Robert F., as quoted in: <u>Congressional Record</u>, vol. 115, November 25, 1969; p. 35877.

27. Moe, Doug, as recorded by Robert Byrne in: <u>The Fourth—And By Far Most Recent—637 Best Things Anybody Ever Said</u>. New York: Atheneum Press, 1990; #402.

28. Roosevelt, Franklin D., Governor of New York, "Looking Forward" Chapter 2, 1933; p. 51.

29. Guest, Edgar A. "It Couldn't Be Done", Verse 1, as recorded in: <u>Edgar A. Guest Says "It Can Be Done"</u>. Chicago: The Reilly & Lee Co., 1938; p. 0.

30. Marcus, Stanley, as quoted by B. Eugene Greissman in: <u>The Achievement Factors</u>. San Marcos, CA: Avant Books/Clawson Communications, Inc., 1990; p. 244.

31. Covey, Stephen R. <u>The 7 Habits of Highly Effective People</u>. New York: Simon and Schuster, 1990; p. 161.

32. Kipling, R. "If—". <u>Rewards and Fairies</u> (1910), as recorded in: <u>Rudyard Kipling's Verse: Inclusive Edition</u>. Garden City, NY: Doubleday, Page & Co., 1927; pp. 645-646.

***** Lewis Kelly, author.

ABOUT THE AUTHOR

Lewis Kelly was born and raised in Butler County, Pennsylvania. He received a B.S. degree in chemistry from Muskingum College in 1965 and a Ph.D. in biochemistry from the University of Pittsburgh in 1970. After serving a number of years on the faculty of the Biochemistry Department at the University of Massachusetts Medical School (Worcester), he joined the National Bladder Cancer Project as Associate Director for Science and then moved to his current position, Associate Director for Administration at the Lucille Parker Markey Cancer Center at the University of Kentucky. "TOIT" is his first non-science work to be published.